Printed in the United States
By Bookmasters

T0171730

CIRCLES OF THE SOUL

A Thoughtful Weekly Experience

MARYMICHELLE LOTANO

Balboa Press books may be ordered through booksellers or by contacting:

Balboa Press
A Division of Hay House
1663 Liberty Drive
Bloomington, IN 47403
www.balboapress.com
1 (877) 407-4847

ISBN: 978-1-4525-1889-3 (sc)
ISBN: 978-1-4525-1888-6 (e)

Library of Congress Control Number: 2014912826

Printed in the United States of America.

Balboa Press rev. date: 08/26/2014

BALBOA.
PRESS
A DIVISION OF HAY HOUSE

INTRODUCTION

It wasn't until I was kneeling before the shards and tiny pieces of a life built on a cracked foundation, that this book began. There was debris everywhere. Some pieces were large and sharp, others were visible but beyond my reach, and still others were completely lost. For a while I insisted I could remake the puzzle in its exact likeness. But I was wrong. My only option was to create a new picture with the pieces that I could salvage on my own. And so I did.

Through the medium of therapeutic art, and the use of color and shape and imagination, I was able to express and reveal my emotions and struggles. I started to let go and grow. My thoughts had room to expose themselves and they became the forefront of my metamorphosis and awakening.

As my eyes fluttered open, and the world took on a different perspective, my thoughts became words. The words and images you are about to experience come from the joy, pain, laughter, tears, smiles, anger, and self love, that we are all capable of experiencing when we open ourselves up to our process and float along with the unexpected.

DEDICATION AND INSPIRATION

This book is dedicated to Trevor who walked with me during my ending.
And to Matt, who pulled me through to my new beginning.

This book was inspired by Yvette Lyons, PhD. who taught me that we can
see and hear and experience the Universe in a myriad of ways.

SPECIAL THANKS

Colette Lannuier – Editing
Yvette Lyons – Cover Art
Christopher Wolfe – Layout Editor and Social Media Coordinator

BEGINNINGS REQUIRE ENDINGS

Can You Learn To Embrace An Ending And Turn It Into A Beginning?

Are we afraid to accept an ending? Do we believe that endings bring only pain and suffering? Is the mess of an ending more than we can bear? Is it more comfortable to be semi conscious in an old story, than vibrant in a new story? Is it possible that the only way to start a new and wondrous life, is by accepting the end of a chapter in our current life?

Everything ends; an awkward moment, a warm smile, an unsettling conversation, an exciting lecture, a sad day, a vacation, a friendship, a love, a marriage, a life. The beauty of every ending is the possibilities that are presented to us on the other side; satisfaction, gratitude, growth, learning, opportunity, rebirth, sorrow, appreciation, and joy.

With each ending we are challenged to find the new beginning. Sometimes our new beginning does not come until we have waded through the sorrow or the grief that comes with closure. And sometimes our new beginning comes immediately, bringing the excitement and change that we have craved. Occasionally our new beginning is unrecognizable, and challenges us to open our perspectives to include something radical and unexpected.

Regardless of the form that each new beginning presents itself to us in, we are pushed and pulled by our spirits to respond and react and engage; and our engagement inevitably changes us. We are forced to include these experiences in our intellect, our emotions, and our psyche. And it is through these encounters, that we become more of who we are meant to be.

ACCEPTANCE ALLOWS US TO BE COMFORTABLE WITH OURSELVES AND THOSE AROUND US

Are You At Peace In The World?

Do we accept that each of us is a unique spiritual being? Can we be comfortable with those who believe differently than we do? Or do we feel the need to change the mind set of others to suit our sense of security?

We all have the ability to accept that there is room for all people and all belief systems within our human existence. Our willingness to be open to differing spiritualities allows us to see that regardless of the manner in which we arrive at our spiritual destinations, all of our souls have the singular purpose to love openly and generously.

By acknowledging that our spirits all have a singular purpose, we gain the awareness that all of our souls originate from a common divine source. In accepting that we all come from one source of love, we can be more tolerant of the varying ways in which each of us access our peace.

But even so, we can sometimes lose sight of our serenity and feel threatened by the different forms of spirituality exhibited by those around us. At these times we have to ask our spirit to assist us in returning to our personal center, so that we can regain our openness toward others and their belief systems.

By returning to a place of inner peace we can embrace the whole of our lives, and let go of the need to control the actions and beliefs of those around us. When we are comfortable with ourselves, then we can feel the depth of our own soul and heed it's purpose. In finding our own spiritual security, we no longer feel the need to change the spiritual path of those around us.

FEAR IS A CHOICE, FIND YOUR VOICE

Are You Afraid To Tackle Your Passions?

Do we allow our fears to silence our voices and reduce our choices? Or do we silence our fears and speak loudly into the world the decisions that reflect our heart's desires?

If we are smart and brave we will always allow ourselves to express our desires and chase after our passions. By choosing our passions, we can overcome our fear and find our true voice.

Because what is fear? Fear is that awful welling that rises up from the bottom of our stomach, and makes our hearts pound and race when we are uncertain of an outcome that we particularly desire or dread. Fear can creep up on us, or it can hit us like a brick. But regardless of the form it arrives in, fear shuts down our logical thought process and our rationale. Our fear disconnects us from our core, our intuition, our psychological mindedness, and our soul. When we are frightened we can no longer access the place we have inside of us tells us all is well.

But fear is natural and normal. Fear is about feeling unsure, feeling insecure, and facing the unknown. When we are in the midst of fear, we have to be willing to open up and ask ourselves why we are afraid to race toward our desires. If we achieve our desires how will our lives be altered? What will our success require of us? How will we respond to failure? If we are willing to answer these questions, then we have started to dissect our fear.

What if on the other side of our fear we find excitement, interest, learning, growing, and our passion? And if we do, then we will have come to the place where our passion can overcome our fear and drive our success every time.

BALANCE BEGETS PEACE

Is There A Synergy Between Your Physical Wellness And Your Spiritual Stability?

What happens when we are psychologically damaged or physically injured? Is it possible to still stand steady in the midst of an emotional upheaval? How do we compensate for a lack of harmony in our lives?

We are a complex triangular system of Spirit, Mind, and Body. For us to be centered and healthy we need to balance the interactions between these systems. It is through the perfect harmony of these systems that we gain peace.

When we lose our stability we can right ourselves if we are willing to examine the opportunity presented to us via our unbalanced triangle. With the happening of an imbalance, we are given an opportunity to examine the broken side and fix it. It is in repairing the damaged piece of our triangle, that we gain wisdom and strength and we regenerate.

Our imbalance is often first seen in the breaking down of our physical body. But when our physical body breaks down, we have to ask ourselves which component is really broken, the spirit, the mind, or the body? Initially, we tend to insist it is the body. But can our emotional and mental challenges manifest themselves in physical symptoms?

When we are physically injured or ill, it is important that we examine where our injury or illness is originating from. We can often be surprised to find that it isn't our body that is injured or ill, but our spirit that is aching, or our mind that is cluttered. And once we gain that awareness, we can focus on strengthening our spirit and clearing our mind, and the physical injury or illness begins to heal concurrently.

OUR FATE LIVES WITHIN US
WE ONLY HAVE TO BE BRAVE ENOUGH
TO SEE IT, AND FEEL IT, AND HEED IT

Does The Courage To Live Out Our Fate
Come From Our Ability To Hear Our Soul Speaking To Us?

The din of our days often drowns out the sound within us, and we become deaf to our intuition. But what do we lose when we cannot hear our inner voice? Do we live our lives at a disadvantage because we cannot hear our soul speaking to us?

When our inner world is loud and distracting, our soul moves through the world cluttered and disengaged. In this state we are unable to fully connect to ourselves. We cannot gain the wisdom that comes from listening to our inner voice.

By quieting ourselves we can learn to hear the sound of our intuition. Through our inner silence we gain the strength, and the wisdom, and the courage we need to live out our fate. Living out our fate requires us to have the strength to see our lives honestly, the wisdom to feel our emotions genuinely, and the courage to act honorably.

As we trust in our fate, and live inside of our strength, our wisdom, and our courage, we learn that we are more than our bodies, more than our intellect, and more than our work. We find that we are now able to live bravely by heeding to a power greater than ourselves. This power allows us to move forward without the benefit of tangible sight, or sound, or touch. In trusting our path, we are able to live out our fate through the guidance of our intuition.

HAS YOUR SOUL FOUND A HOME YET...
AND IF IT HAS, HAVE YOU LET IT UNPACK?

Is Life Destiny, Or Decision, Or The Combination Of Both?

Destiny is an inevitable experience or encounter, with a person or a place, that we are meant to intersect with during the course of our lifetime. A decision is the action of determining if we will participate in the event, or the relationship, that we are presented with.

During the course of our lifetime we face many choices that change our circumstances and introduce us to our challenges. Are these events random, or planned, or a combination of both? What if we are faced with a destination, or a person, that we refuse to encounter and engage with? Do we change the course of our lives for the better or the worse with our decision making power?

Our life experiences twist and turn and guide us through a miraculous combination of destiny and decision. Through the power of time and timing, we are always safely delivered to the places, events, and people, that our souls are meant to encounter. Through our gift of conscious and logical thought, we are able to reason and determine how we will engage in, and react to, our arrival at these destinations and our encounters with these souls.

If we close our hearts to these destined moments, we stagnate and force ourselves on a new and different path. But when we open our hearts and embrace the crossings of our path, we become vulnerable to what these destinations and souls have to offer us. It is in our willingness to engage in our truest plan, that allows our soul finds it's most treasured resting places.

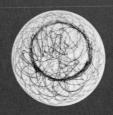

BE KIND, GIVE GENEROUSLY, LIVE GENUINELY

Can You Intertwine Kindness And Generosity
To Create A More Genuine World?

We all believe that we are kind and generous. It is rare that we meet someone who professes to be mean and stingy. And yet, do we feel the kindness that people profess to put into the world? Do we feel safe and fulfilled by receiving the unconditional generosity of strangers, acquaintances, friends, and family? And if we do not feel this type of openness and love in our lives, is it because we do not put it out there to be returned to us? Are we responsible for leading with our kindness and generosity?

If we want something from the world we must first be vulnerable enough to step forward and place it quietly and lovingly into the world so that it can be returned to us. Many might disagree with this and respond that they will not contribute until they see some tangible proof that the world will return their kindness and generosity. But instead, we can choose to step forward with our kindness and our generosity and make a deposit. From that simple action, we have begun the chain of living genuinely.

When we step forward with our most genuine self, we arrive at a place where we can finally be open to receiving all forms of goodness. And this is where we can begin to experience fulfillment from the actions of strangers, acquaintances, friends, and family. Kindness, generosity, and genuineness is always available to us. It is always waiting for us to invite it in. We simply have to open the door.

WHEN WE SPEAK THE TRUTH, THE REACTION OF OTHERS IS NOT ABOUT US

What Type Of Truth Is Worth Speaking?

Are we allowed to speak a truth that is painful, or are we only supposed to speak a truth that is easily accepted by the recipient? Do we shy away from speaking that which is true, but unpleasant? Is there a way that we can impart an unwelcomed truth without inducing another's defenses?

Truth can be a very slippery bedfellow. Truth is subject to our perception and the perception of the one being spoken to. It is also subject to interpretation and misperception. Everyone has a version of their own truth as it relates to the words and actions they place into the world.

We all know our inner truth. It is only our ego that colors our willingness to understand and admit to the truth behind our motivations and subsequent words and actions. And while we may believe that we are aware of the thoughts and motivations behind all of our actions, we are rarely correct about this.

If we want to have a full awareness of our truth, and the courage to voice our truth, we must sit in silence and find our truth. When we sit in silence our truth bubbles to the surface and we find a greater depth of understanding about ourselves and our intentions. Once we understand the true intentions behind our words and our actions, we are able to speak our truth without causing another person harm.

AWARENESS CANNOT BE ERASED
ONLY IGNORED

Where Do You Hide Your Awareness?

Are we cognizant of the whole of who we are in the world? Or are we only concerned with paying attention to those situations that we are comfortable with? Are we brave enough to be aware of the things that make us anxious or fearful, or will require us to drastically change ourselves and our environment?

Being aware of the ordinary experiences of our lives is easy. We handle these occurrences without any disruption to our days. Our awareness presents us with no challenge or discomfort. In these instances we proceed on a comfortable path to success and joy.

But being aware of the things that frighten us, or require us to change, demands much more from us. This type of awareness challenges us to act with faith and courage. If we are conscious of the forms of awareness that require us to move or change or grow, do we accept the challenge, or do we walk away?

If we are brave, we do not walk away from our awareness. We engage in our mindfulness and accept our challenges. Because even in our greatest discomfort, our awareness can not be erased. By refusing to be acknowledge the things that are more disruptive to our lives, we short ourselves the chance to be more than we ever anticipated we could be.

If we incorporate our awareness into our life, then we create the chance to succeed or fail. Both of these outcomes can lead to greatness, and the opportunity to wake up our expectations to a happiness that we might not have anticipated.

OUR CHALLENGES ALLOW US TO DEFINE OURSELVES, THEY DO NOT DEFINE US

How Do You Approach Your Struggles?

We are challenged every day. Sometimes our challenges are ordinary and include nothing more than getting ourselves and our family out of the house with clean teeth and in clean clothes. These are not the types of challenges that we give much credence to, because they do not slow us down.

But what happens when we are faced with challenges that do slow us down, or become chronic, or even seemingly insurmountable? In these moments or days or years, we have an opportunity to define ourselves. And what will the definition of our essence be? Will we present ourselves as strong, tired, weak, stoic, inflexible, open, humorous, accepting, bitter, quiet, or relentless? Will we show the world our smile or our tears?

If we are honest with ourselves, we will acknowledge that we will exhibit a range of emotions and behaviors in response to our struggles. Some of our emotions will remain private. Some of our behaviors will not change. Some of our emotions will spill into our place of work or study. Some of our behaviors may surprise us and others. We may not be able to fully control every emotion or behavior that surfaces. And we may emerge a seemingly different person.

But the type of new person we emerge as, is entirely up to us.

ENERGY FLOWS WHERE ATTENTION GOES

What Do You Choose To Focus On?

Every day there is a plethora of demands for our time and attention. Sometimes we give our time without giving our focus. Often we want to give more attention to events or people, but we cannot find more time to give. As a result, we often feel torn and depleted and inadequate.

What are those things in our lives that are significant and warrant more of our time and attention? How do we remedy our inability to give our energy to those things that truly matter?

First we have to define what truly matters to us. It is different for everyone. For some, it is being available to wake their children and take them to school, or to read them a bedtime story. For others, it is being able to give their talents to a particular aspect of their career. And for many, it is the need to place their energy equally with friends, family, and work.

But simply identifying where our energy needs to flow, does not solve the dilemma of whether we can actually move our energy in that specified and focused direction. To do so we often have to make choices.

What will you have to leave by the wayside to be truly present for
the events and the people that are significant to you?

MAY WE BE BLESSED WITH THE COURAGE TO CHOOSE OUR SOUL'S DESTINY

Does Your Soul Have Its Own Unique Plan For Growth?

If you ask people if they are growing they are likely to respond by saying, "I stopped growing when I was 19. I've been this size ever since." But what about our psychological, intellectual, and spiritual growth? Is there an age limit on the maturation of these pieces of the human mind and soul?

For some, there is. We all know people who do not expand. And while it might be tempting to suggest they experiment with change and growth, it might not be well received. Because when it comes to soul growth, it must be an intrinsically motivated journey.

All souls have a unique growth plan. But in order for each soul's plan to reach its full potential, we have to be ready to say yes to the unexpected. It is through the unexpected person or event that we have to think quickly, change radically, or show our vulnerability. Thinking quickly might mean taking advantage of a spontaneous proposal, changing radically might mean physically moving ourselves to a new location, and showing our vulnerability might mean becoming emotionally immersed with another soul.

When we say yes to an unexpected crossroad, we open ourselves up to mature and to grow in an unanticipated way. And if we welcome an unexpected event or person into our lives, then we might find ourselves, and our soul, in a state of immense pleasure, as it's own unique plan unfolds.

EXPERIENCE IS WHAT YOU GET WHEN YOU DON'T GET WHAT YOU WANT

How Often Do You Believe That You Know
What Is Right For You and
Your Future?

We all have times when we want a particular outcome or a particular relationship in our lives, and so we ask that our desires be delivered to us. Sometimes the answer to our demands is yes. But often the answer to our requests is no. What do we learn when the answer is yes verses no?

When the answer to our deepest desires is yes, we move through the experience with joy and a sense of satisfaction. We tell ourselves that we knew what was best for us and we were correct. Very often, this is where our thought process ends. We have what we want.

But what happens when the response to our wish is no? How do we react when we don't get the job that we had hoped for, or the gift that we were coveting, or our feelings are not reciprocated by the person that we believed would be the perfect fit for us?

In each of these circumstances we face disappointment and sorrow. Sometimes we feel despair because we are sure that we know what is best for us. Often we cannot open ourselves up to recognizing that we have just been given the gift of experience.

The experience that comes with disappointment is finding our fortitude, the experience that comes with sorrow is finding our grace, and the experience that comes with despair is finding our hope. Through the gifts of fortitude, grace, and hope we are privileged with the opportunity to discover that a perceived misfortune can lead to a spectacular outcome.

CHANGE THE RULES THAT KEEP YOU
IN THE DARK AND SHINE

What Rules Are You Afraid To Change Or Break?

Society places many expectations on us. We are pressured to move through our life in a certain order; grow up, become educated, develop a career, engage in a relationship, build a family, be committed, and age gracefully. But there are times when circumstances beg us to shine in a different direction.

What do we do if we are in the midst of a particular path and we are presented with a new opportunity? Do we dare to stray? If we stray, will we succeed? If we do not stray, will we dim our star?

We are a part of this world to shine. Oftentimes we become dull and disenchanted with our path and our surroundings because we have forgotten that it is our own choices that brought us to a seemingly dissatisfying destination. On these days, it behooves us to shake ourselves and blink away the darkness. We need to clear our sight and our minds of our self imposed restrictions, and reconnect with our passions.

In reconnecting with our passions we remember that we are unique. We discover that we have something spectacular to present to those around us. And we realize that it is an honor to take our place in the world and sparkle.

SILENCE IS WISDOM

What Can You Learn From Silencing Your Voice, Quieting Your Mind,
And Opening Your Heart?

We are not a society that embraces silence. Throughout our day we are continually infiltrated with some type of sound. We are constantly within range of human conversation, or music, or the sound of our television, or the traffic around us. As a result of such an intense amount of noise, we rarely silence our voices, or our minds, or our hearts, long enough to understand what other people are trying to communicate to us.

When we silence our voices, we can engage in listening to the content of the conversation that we are participating in. When we quiet our minds, we can comprehend the genuine needs of those around us with greater depth. And when we open our hearts, we are privy to the emotional quotient of the experience of the moment.

By incorporating these skills into our daily lives we are better able to receive the true meaning of the messages people are trying to impart to us. By silencing our voices, and quieting our minds, and engaging our hearts, we become more sensitive to the subtleties of the communications we partake in. It is through our silence and sensitivity that we gain the wisdom that comes from being present to hear and experience another human beings story.

BIRTHDAYS ARE THE GIFT OF A SOUL

How Do You Celebrate Your Arrival Into This Magnificent World?

When we are young celebrating our birthday is something wonderful and exciting. We await it's arrival with excited anticipation and greet it with unbridled enthusiasm. We embrace aging, and all of the trimmings of cake and candles and hugs and kisses and gifts and balloons, with joy and passion.

But as we grow older we lose our sense of wonder and begin to approach our aging with dread and dissatisfaction. We tend to use this magnificent and natural marker of time as a flogging stick for all of the things we have not yet accomplished. We admonish our changing bodies, try to scrub away our wrinkles of wisdom, and ignore the maturity that comes with the arrival of our subscription to AARP magazine.

Instead, maybe it is time to cuddle up to our years and their true meaning. In the years that we have come through, we have shown our strength and grown in our character. We have shown our compassion and grown in expressing our empathy. We have shown our intuition and grown in exhibiting our trust. We have shown our stability and grown in our predictability. We have shown our self esteem and grown in our self confidence. We have shown our love and grown in our ability to open our hearts. We have shown our kind thoughts and grown in our ability to express our kind words. We have shown our spirituality and grown in our peace of mind.

And we now have been given a moment to reflect on these years and to commit ourselves to another year of change and learning and inspiration.

So let's CELEBRATE!

OUR SCARS HEAL WITH CONNECTION

How Do You Recover From Your Pain and Mend Your Heart?

Because we are feeling beings we inevitably experience pain both physically and emotionally. Our physical pain is often relieved with medication, and our body heals or returns to a homeostatic state with minimal effort on our part. Yet it is not always so easy to remedy our emotional pain. Emotional distress comes from a variety of ordinary human experiences. We often succumb to emotional strain as a result of disappointment, abandonment, rejection, and abuse.

When we find ourselves struggling because our emotional expectations have not been met, it is easy to withdraw and withhold ourselves from others. We tell ourselves that we do not want to risk the anguish that comes from not being loved or accepted for who we are, and what we have to offer another person. But if we confine ourselves to this stance, we cannot move freely toward new people.

The only way to grow past our discomfort is to step out of it and reach beyond it. When we connect ourselves to those around us by sharing our pain, we realize that we are not alone. We find others who have the lived with the same vulnerabilities and fears. It is through our common emotional experiences that we gain empathy and compassion and tolerance.

As we connect and intertwine our lives with those around us, we lessen our aloneness and begin to heal. It is through our ability to connect that we find the courage to risk our emotions and start anew. It is in starting anew that our scars begin to fade, and our pain begins to recede. And when our pain recedes, our heart begins to mend.

SOMETIMES WE ONLY GET A MOMENT TO MAKE OUR GREATEST DESIRES COME TRUE; BE READY, BE BRAVE, SPEAK UP

Will You Speak Up?

Sometimes we listen to a lecture and the content resonates with us. Sometimes we read an article and the subject matter stirs a strong dissenting opinion in us. Sometimes we participate in a public or educational system that perpetrates a lack of logic in its policies. What is our response to being inspired, or agitated, or driven to interject our common sense into the equation?

If we are aware of our own desire for growth and change in our lives, then we can also be ready to engage in action that moves us toward turning our convictions into our reality. To do this we have to be ready, be brave, and speak up.

We can be ready by being present in all that we do, so that our experiences are alive with thought and action. We can be brave by acknowledging that pushing ourselves outside of our comfort zone, takes courage. And we can speak up once we have successfully coupled our awareness and our daring, into a coherent plan for transformation.

If we refuse to seize the moment when all three of these dynamics come together, then we will miss our opportunity to make a difference, in even the smallest matter, which can be of the greatest importance.

LIFE IS NOT ABOUT SHORT TERM COMFORT
IT IS ABOUT LONG TERM BALANCE

How Do You Balance Your Scale?

Our days are a complex mix of several components. We have to attend to our work, our home, our family, our relationships, our physical health, our emotional stability, and our spiritual growth. The demands of all of these responsibilities weigh upon us and divides our time and attention.

On a good day we have the energy to give adequately to each of these slices of life. On a difficult day we may find ourselves tipping the scale in favor of a particular pressing need. If we give too much, or too infrequently, to a particular section of our life, we can find ourselves gaining comfort for the moment, but jeopardizing our overall balance.

Balance is knowing that we cannot give too much or too little to one aspect of our existence. If we give everything to work for prestige or monetary gain, we lose our relationships. If we give everything to our family, we lose our perspective on the workings of the outside world. If we focus all of our time on our emotional stability and spiritual growth, we forget to engage with those around us. If we neglect our physical health, we deplete the energy and enthusiasm of our body and our mind.

We need to remember to take the time to flow equally and smoothly in and out of the physical, emotional, and spiritual portals that shape our days. By doing so we balance our energy and our attention, and create harmony in our lives.

BE MORE…

Can You Be More…?

Caring
Loving, Generous
Discerning, Gracious, Giving
Intelligent, Curious, Forgiving, Flattering
Participating, Open, Adventurous, Joyous, Profound
Curious, Aware, Flamboyant, Soft, Empathetic, Compassionate
Patient, Exciting, Expressive, Beloved, Incandescent, Prepared, Kind
Spiritual, Soulful, Fulfilled, Solid, Trusting, Peaceful, Predictable,
Thoughtful, Insightful, Learned, Stimulating, Leisurely,
Quiet, Hearty, Determined, Persistent, Musical,
Enriched, Resilient, Decisive, Awake
Silent, Contemplative, Reflective
Quirky, Grateful, Tranquil
Magnificent, Amazing
Spectacular!

BRAVERY...IT DEFINES US

How Big Is Your Brave?

When we think of bravery we often conjure up the most obvious thoughts of our men and women in the armed forces, our police officers, our firefighters, and our paramedics. Then we might consider our doctors and nurses and the people who engage in humanitarian efforts around the world. Our immediate frame of reference always slides to those who put themselves in physical danger every day for the welfare of others.

But what about the small singular acts of bravery that happen every day? What about those fighting terminal illnesses, or children who live in neglectful situations and still manage to go to school every day, or women who escape the bondage of abuse, or those who decide to risk a career change, or those who open up to a new relationship, or those who are willing to speak an unpopular truth?

Being brave is about making a decision and taking an action, without the advantage of a known secure and safe outcome. When we are brave we risk our physical security, and we expose our emotional truth, thereby placing ourselves in the zone of the unknown consequence.

Bravery changes us. We are now a person who has contemplated and ventured and altered ourselves, or someone else, by our conduct or our statements. As a result we can no longer define ourselves by our past behaviors or rhetoric. Our bravery has redefined us.

IF YOU WANT TO BE LOVED
CUDDLE YOUR UGLY

What Is The Most Unattractive Part Of Who You Are?

It is very unusual that anyone ever questions us about the least desirable parts of who we are. And even more rare, is how infrequently we acknowledge our own most unappealing traits.

What would happen if we made a list of our most awful thoughts and feelings and behaviors? Do we wish that the people who get in our way would simply disappear? Do we resist our unpleasant feelings so that we do not have to admit that we don't like someone we are supposed to love? Are we willing to accept that we use our actions to manipulate people, or situations, to secure our own desired outcomes? But is it possible that acknowledging this side of us would free us from believing that we are perfect, and allow us to accept our flaws and the flaws of others? Would we then be able to move forward with more compassion, love, and authenticity?

When we refuse to own our ugly thoughts or feelings or behaviors, we are not genuine with ourselves. If we are disingenuous with knowing ourselves, we cannot engage in an honest relationship that will allow people to love us for exactly who we are. And if we refuse to see the unattractive parts of the people we engage with, we cannot love them for the true people they are. The feelings we have for them are then conditional, and based only upon the personality traits that we are willing to see in them, or those that we have projected onto them.

We must be authentic in defining who we are. And we must be willing to see others for who they really are. Only when we genuinely accept ourselves for who we are, and others for their true self, can we give and receive unconditional love.

OUR EMOTIONAL SECRETS
RARELY REMAIN SECRETS FOREVER

How Do Your Emotional Secrets Reveal Themselves?

We tend to believe that admitting and revealing our emotional secrets is a choice we make, not an inevitability. But what if that notion is incorrect? What if we were to acknowledge that the truth of our feelings is always available for our awareness? How would that make us more responsible for our own sincerity, and the degree of candor we bring to our relationships with other people?

If we refuse to acknowledge or accept our emotional secrets, we might be able to remain inside of an unsatisfying work or personal choice indefinitely. In declining to recognize or define our dissatisfaction, we can proceed from day to day without indentifying the need to make a change that could place our lives in a tailspin.

Yet despite our best efforts, we can find the foundation of our emotional fortress cracking under the pressure of a hidden truth. Our ability to ignore a negative feeling, or a lack of feeling, or an overall sense of dissatisfaction in our work or personal life, can surface with an intensity that is impossible to deny. It is within this emotional shift that change happens without our consent.

When we are faced with accepting a necessary self-realization, we have an opportunity to evolve and expand our understanding of ourselves and our lives. In being open to our own truths, we allow new perspectives to enter our consciousness. Once we are willing to examine our emotions and our thoughts under a different microscope, we grow into a more learned and enlightened individual.

"CREATIVITY CHANGES THE WORLD"

MATT SANDERS

If You Put Your Ideas Into Action Would They
Be The Change The World Needs?

Do we carefully consider what our responsibilities are for changing the world? Is it necessary for us to alter our community on a grand scale in order to make an impact? Or can we instigate a difference by changing our approach toward a single person, thereby having a profound effect on that individual and their overtures toward others?

We often spend our day in a state of creative mediocrity. As we slide through the day attending to our work, our family, and ourselves, we tend to repeat our behavioral patterns. In approaching our life in this manner we become numb to the idea of incorporating new approaches into our ordinary encounters. And while this is an effective maintenance strategy, it causes us to become dull and disconnected.

To approach the world with creativity requires us to generate one original act in response to an ordinary occurrence or problem. In doing so we fashion a new set of circumstances that allows us to interact with people in a fresh way. Once we relate to those around us in a different way, we change our connections to them, and deepen our relationships with them.

Our responsibility for making the world a more interesting adventure simply requires us to reach into our imagination, combine it with our knowledge, and free our creativity.

BE AT PEACE WITH THE HUM AND THE SWAY

Can You Accept And Thrive In The Place You Are At In Your Life At This Exact Moment?

How often have we said to ourselves or to others, "Everything would be fine if…" What does this statement say about us and our ability to live inside of our current life circumstances? Are we ungrateful? Are we greedy? Do we believe we are entitled to more than we are immediately blessed with?

Because we live in a world of material abundance, we rarely want for the comfort of food, shelter, or currency. We may feel we do not have enough of these items, but it is uncommon that we are actually deprived of these necessities. In our emotional, psychological, and spiritual lives, we might also be yearning for more, and yet nothing significant is forthcoming.

Every day we are asked to accept the place we wake up to. Sometimes it is a place of peace and joy and total fulfillment, and we gladly move ourselves into what awaits us. At other times we wake up and wonder how it is possible that anyone, or any higher guide, could possibly expect us to put our feet on the floor and step knowingly into the challenges that confront us. In either scenario, we are forced to focus and function.

And we do, because we have to. It is that simple and that complex. The decisive factor is whether we believe that we are in the moment for our greater good, or for a period of extended suffering. If we believe that we are in the moment for a period of agony, then we will only see darkness in the day. But if we choose to be in the moment for our greater good, then we can have faith in the hum of the lesson of the day, and we can trust in the gentle sway that pulls us toward our intended future.

YOU CAN'T DO LIFE FOR SOMEONE
BUT YOU CAN BE THERE TO DO LIFE WITH SOMEONE

Are You Able To Let Others Be?

Do we have the patience to allow others to wander down their own path? Can we be silent even if someone we love is making a decision that we do not see the logic in? Are we willing to step back and let people choose their dreams, even if their choice seems foolish to us?

In many of our relationships we find ourselves trying to coerce others into following our lead. Sometimes we refuse to allow people to make their own choices by continually asking them to change their minds. In a worst case scenario, we will try to actually make decisions for others. In our relationships with our co-workers we will want our colleagues to get on board with our sense of project development. As spouses we expect our partner to participate in the same events that we enjoy. And as parents we move our children to excel and succeed in the areas that we believe are important.

We need to remember that we all have the right to yield to our own intuition when choosing our way. Sometimes we have been where the person we love is choosing to go and our outcome was less than desirable, so we scream, "Don't Go There!"

But wouldn't it be more fruitful if instead we said, "Be brave, take the risk, the outcome might fit you well!" Because isn't it our own greatest hope that when we are ready to leap, that the people we love will support our journey and cheer for our achievements?

Our freedom to scribe our own adventure is a divine gift. So when those around us are writing their story,

LET THE BROKEN PIECES GO

Do You Hold Onto Your Pain Long After The Expiration Date?

When is the right time to fully forgive someone who has had a negative impact on your emotional existence? Does forgiving require us to also forget the incident and its ramifications? Is it possible that we can be left with a scar that simply will not recede?

No one leaves this life without hurting someone or being hurt by someone. Emotional pain is the quintessential human experience. We have all spoken or behaved in ways that has caused someone else to feel the sting of rejection or embarrassment. And we have all had the same perpetrated upon us.

But sometimes, even after the apologies have been exchanged and we have forgiven those who hurt us, we are left with a residual pang of pain. The remains of the experience can take root within us and cause us to live with a heightened sense of caution, or even a palpable fear of emotionally investing in others. When we sidle up with our wariness and shrink from engagement, we close ourselves off from connection.

Continuing to embrace our scars jeopardizes our vulnerability. By holding onto our broken pieces, we ensnare our ability to be open to attachment. Because what are our broken pieces? They are the jagged emotional edges that create a barrier between us and others. They make us sharp and unapproachable. But if we let our broken piece go, we can create a new space that can be filled by a softer and more loving experience.

WE ALL NEED SOMEONE TO WALK AHEAD OF US IN LIFE
SO THAT WHEN WE NEED HELP
THEY CAN SLOW DOWN,
OFFER US A HAND,
AND WALK ALONG WITH US

Are You Walking Ahead Or Reaching Forward?

Have you ever watched a friend or loved one struggle through a life changing event and then found yourself in the same set of circumstances, looking to them for guidance? Have you ever had to reach back to give someone a hand up because your life experiences gave insight and comfort to a person who was just one step behind you?

In each lifetime there are lessons for our souls to learn that are inherent to our humanity. Some souls learn their lessons quickly and efficiently. Other souls struggle to master the basics of growth. But regardless of where our soul is, it is always in a state of anticipated change. Every soul has something to learn from someone ahead of them, or something to offer to someone behind them.

We are meant to pull and push each other through our encounters in each existence that we participate in. Some of us have engaged in several lifetimes and are mainly pull souls. Others of us are new to the human adventure and need to be reaching forward to expand and conquer our chosen assignments.

No matter what our position is, we are meant to assist and guide and encourage and support one another. Each time we respond to someone in need, or receive an encouraging word, we need to celebrate that we have just achieved a soul objective and balanced our spiritual account.

INTEGRITY IS SHOWING THE WORLD YOUR KNOWN TRUTH

How Do Your Actions Define Your Integrity?

Integrity is accurately reflecting the whole of who we are to the world we inhabit. It is putting our honesty, our fairness, our kindness, and our genuineness on display for all to experience.

When our integrity is pleasant, we are welcomed by others. If we are keeping our word to give someone a ride, or arriving on time for lunch, or babysitting someone's children, we are greeted with enthusiasm. Our dependability and kindness has made someone else's life easier.

However when we place the whole of our integrity into the arena of our every day life, our honor is not always attractive to those around us. Our integrity may be poorly received if we are being forthright and speaking a truth that no one wants to hear. Sometimes our probity will demand that we change a behavior that is dysfunctional to us, but integral those who engage with us.

It is easy for us to showcase our integrity when the action we need to take lies cleanly and clearly inside of social expectations. But it can be a challenge to live by our honor when the situation dares us to place our virtue on the ledge of an unpleasant reality. It is our genuineness and our grace under the pressure of these circumstances, that reveals the depth of our integrity.

OUR PERCEPTIONS PRECEDE US

When You Express Your Perception Of The World, Do You Effect Tolerance In The World?

Do we believe that our perception of the world is the most accurate? Are we tolerant of other people's perspectives? Are we careful and respectful when expressing our perceptions of the world to others?

We sense the world through three mediums that are unique to each of us. Through our spirit, we connect to others in the world. Through our mind, we gain an intellectual understanding of the world. And as a human body, we move through the world. As we gain our perspective of the world through this trio, we then express our perceptions to those around us.

By expressing our perceptions, and experiencing the reactions of others, we then choose whether we will welcome someone into our life, or move across the room from them. This decision is contingent upon the alignment of our spirit, mind, and body to theirs. The key to harmonizing our perspective of the world with another individuals, is to fully connect with a person in the spirit, mind, and body, simultaneously.

Simultaneous connections soften our hearts, enlighten our minds, and stimulate our bodies. It is this emotional, intellectual, and physical reciprocity that allows us to understand each others perception of the world. When we understand another person's perception of the world, we are able to empathize with them. Empathizing with another human being creates tolerance in us, and allows us to bring tolerance into the world.

WHEN THERE ARE LIES AT THE CORE, WE CONTAMINATE EVERYTHING THAT STEMS THERE FROM

Can You Begin Each Adventure From Your Truth?

Is there a battle between our image and our core truth? Are we able to express ourselves with honesty from the inception of each relationship we step into? Is there a difference if we begin with an omission of who we are, verses beginning with a misrepresentation of who we are?

From the moment we shake hands with someone new we set a relationship into motion. It may be a relationship that only lasts for the duration of a cocktail party, or it could be a connection that lasts a lifetime. But either way, the quality of the experience we engage in will be driven by the hub of who we are.

If the center of our relationships is contaminated by a false impression of who we are, then every aspect of that association is tainted. By hiding our true self, we deny the person we are engaged with the opportunity to genuinely know us. When we are not exposed to the most authentic version of the people we invite into our lives, then we are thwarted the chance to accept someone for all that they have to offer.

We are always at an advantage when we place our most authentic self into the world. In doing so we create and exchange with others our purest essence. When we are at our purest, our beauty can be experienced honestly and totally.

RISK REWARDS US

Can You Embrace The Benefits Of Both Success and Failure?

When we think of taking a risk our mind immediately conjures up images of cliff diving, running category four rapids, swimming with sharks, or even ingesting a dozen cupcakes in one sitting. Yet risk does not have to be big. We risk success and failure with a multitude of decisions and behaviors that we make or engage in on a regular basis.

The first step toward taking a risk is awareness, the second step toward taking a risk is acceptance, and the final step toward taking a risk is openness. Risk is not about being impulsive, it is about conscious thought and decision making.

Therefore, We Risk When

We express a new thought; Take a new job
Make a new friend; Have a baby
Try a new hair cut; Fall in love
Start exercising; Throw a party
Go back to school; Travel
Volunteer; Argue
Move; Divorce

Each time we risk venturing into a new arena, we can either succeed or fail. When we succeed we experience a sense of self-esteem, growth, movement, and completion. When we fail we are privy to indentifying our self-determination, experiencing contemplation, re-evaluating our position, and finding our perseverance. But whatever our final outcome is, we are rewarded with adding a new dimension to our humanity.

ATTRACTION IS NOT OPTIONAL

Do You Choose Who You Love?

We tend to believe that we have control over how we feel about the people we encounter. Some people we like, and others we do not. It seems very simple and well within our choosing. But is it? Are we connected to some people beyond our immediate understanding and decision making power? Do our souls recognize a choice we made long before we fell into our human form? And does this choice manifest itself in our feeling states, beyond our intellect and rationale?

Many people do not have a burning desire to answer these questions. And most people will not even entertain these issues. However, we have all experienced attractions that we might not have welcomed into our lives, and yet we could not resist them.

When we are pulled toward the inexplicable magnetism of another individual, we find ourselves compelled to respond. Depending upon the circumstances we may initially greet the experience with resistance. But our resistance is usually thwarted by the intense nature of the energy we feel pulling us toward the energy of another. We seem to know that we have something we need to learn or experience, by participating in the particular relationship.

When the components of physical and emotional attraction clink into place, our experience is heightened and the desire to engage in the relationship is overwhelming. It is the coming together of these powerful attractions that opens us up to the chance of enriching ourselves, by exploring the excitement of an unanticipated intimacy.

WHAT IF EVERY STEP OF EVERY DAY WAS TAKEN WITH DIGNITY...AND KINDNESS...AND COURAGE
WHAT IF?

How Do You Approach Your Day?

Every morning when we open our eyes and our first thoughts are...

I'm late, I'm tired, I'm behind
I hate traffic, I hate work, I hate email
My children need lunches, money, and homework
The dog needs to be fed, to go out, and to get to daycare
I will have to make dinner, clean the kitchen, and do the laundry

We then put our feet on the floor and we take our first three steps into the day cranky, annoyed, and depleted. We are off to a miserable start.

What if every morning when we open our eyes our first thoughts are...

I'm alive, I'm well, I'm rested
The dog is loving, gentle, and fun
My children are healthy, smart, and safe
I am able bodied, I am financially secure, I am connected
I will nourish my family, be thankful for shelter, and appreciate warmth

From here we can put our feet onto the floor and take our first three steps into the day grateful, compassionate, and brave. We are off to a magnificent start.

RUN...HOME

Imagine If You Knew That Tomorrow Was Your Last Day,
Who Would You Run To?

Then run in that direction today. What are you waiting for? Whatever it is, you don't need it. You need to move.

Forward
Today

In our every day state of self induced stoicism, we tend to forget that we have the power to move, to change, to grow, to renew, to repair, to reach out, and to love. Instead we stagnate in our intimacies with others. We stop running toward one another. We shut down our willingness communicate. We withdraw from expressing our truest emotions. And we begin to shrivel from sentiment.

But we have the ability to reconnect to those that we are already bound to, or to reach out for new pathways to devotion and joy. Our will is free to choose the unique encounters that excite us and motivate us toward fresh relationships, and interesting experiences. We are unencumbered in the myriad of ways we can grow and change, in relation to those we invite to share in our lives.

We should not wait to run toward our sense of home. Every moment is a chance to be on the move in the direction of true connection with those we love. We are free to do this on any given day.

Is Today Your Given Day?

PUT YOUR DEMONS DOWN

How Forgiving Are You Of Your Choices Gone Awry?

A mistake. An error in judgment. A decision turned destructive. An unexpected outcome. A dark moment. Have you let these consequences go, or is your backpack of burdens bursting at the seams?

A mistake is a bad return on an investment of time, thought, emotion, or money. Our inability to accurately evaluate a circumstance and its potential outcome, can cause us great angst and sorrow. We find ourselves questioning our intelligence, logic, intuition, and wisdom. And when it is a mistake of epic proportions, we tend to expend a disproportionate amount of time and energy reviewing that split second where it all went horribly wrong.

But there comes a day or a night, when we have to pardon ourselves and move on. If we refuse to do so, we remain grounded in our misdoing and frozen in time. Our ongoing view of the world is colored by negativity and doubt.

Once we have analyzed, and mulled, and rolled, and cuddled, and cried, and screamed, and wished, and prayed, and bargained, and begged, for the understanding and the reasoning, behind a devastating outcome, it is time to accept the learning and lose the loss. It is time to put our demons down.

SOLUTIONS COME WITH CONNECTION
NOT CONFRONTATION

Do You Solve Your Problems With Honey Or Vinegar?

We are a conflict oriented society. We are quick to argue with those who do not give us what we want. We use technology to scream our demands to large audiences. We drive and fight with those who travel near us. We use our legal system to avenge every possible injustice presented to us. When we storm through the world ready for a fight, the world returns the favor by presenting us with a war.

But what if we changed our approach to confrontation? What if we stopped talking and started listening to the other participant? What if we were present and available, emotionally and psychologically, to ascertain the circumstances surrounding the conflict? What if we considered someone else's feelings, before presenting our anger and frustration?

Approaching the more cantankerous side of life with something sweeter than verbal venom, can lead us to solutions that are more peaceful. Finding our empathy and reacting with our compassion, can lead us to agreements that perpetuate understanding and wisdom. Expressing our ideas in a calm and careful manner, can lead us to resolutions that are creative and innovative.

When we change our reaction to strife, we alter the dynamic of the event. By altering one side of the energy, the other side must shift also. Once we shift the force of the exchange, we have the opportunity to morph the solution into an occasion that can also create a connection.

DISMISS THE DECEPTION...DIVE INTO THE TRUTH...
FIND THE PEACE...REVEL IN THE JOY

Is Denial Your Permanent Address?

We all deceive ourselves. Usually it is for self-protection because we are afraid to acknowledge our true circumstances. Mindfulness might require us to change our situation. If we are not ready for change, we tend to bury our awareness. Our choice to do so can be purposeful and necessary and serve us well, for a limited time. But our engagement with our truth is eventually calendared for revelation.

When we consent to tumble into the truth, we chance that our new found breakthroughs will require us to expand our horizons in a direction where the light is dim, or non-existent. The mere thought of a journey with an unidentified destination, can cause us to want to turn back.

But if we stop and allow our truth to resonate with us, we will find that our truth brings us peace of mind and calmness of spirit. We will recognize that we do know where we are going, even if the final outcome is not visible.

As we allow ourselves to move forward using our truth and our peace as our guide, we find a new beginning. In finding a new beginning our perception of ourselves is altered, and our interaction with the world expands. By expanding our interaction with ourselves and others, we gain wisdom and enlightenment, thereby creating the opportunity to revel in the joy that comes with the culmination of following an unanticipated path.

WE RE-PAIR TO REPAIR

When Is It Time For Your Soul To Re-Mate?

Do we always recognize our soul mates? Is it possible we could confuse a learning partner with a true soul mate? What happens when we outgrow a learning partner? And if we do recognize our soul mates, are we always willing to pair ourselves with them?

Society and religion teach us that we are to pair for a lifetime, and we are to remain paired with our original choice through thick and thin. We are not allowed to openly enter into our legal and religious relationships, with the understanding that we will only stay committed to one another for the period that the relationship nourishes our soul growth. Instead we are expected to struggle and strive, and fight and cling, and remain bonded and eternally enslaved to our original selection, regardless of the nature of the engagement.

But sometimes we are knee-deep in a relationship that no longer carries any connection for us. This circumstance creates a gap in our lives and leaves us open and hungry for change and emotional maturation. It is precisely at this juncture that the Universe will deliver to us a chance to rearrange our lives with a new human energy.

And this is where free will takes over. After you have recognized the other half of your current self inside of someone else's eyes, what do you do? Do you insist that you did not see it? Do you see it, and turn and walk the other way? Or do you move heaven and earth to remain inside of that gaze for the duration of your soul plan?

What Will You Do?

THE POWER OF POTENTIAL IS POTENT

What Do You Have To Offer?

When we think of potential we immediately focus on the positive aspects of what we are capable of achieving for ourselves, and offering to others. We rarely consider that we are also capable of delivering less desirable actions and words to a situation. These less desirable behaviors can showcase our potential to be unkind and selfish, or uncooperative and destructive.

There are days when we arrive at an event with a mindset that has the ability to bring forth negativity and criticism. Maybe we escort these attitudes to the table because we are tired or angry or irritated with a personality, or an issue, that we are being required to work with. But when we approach our involvements from this vantage point, our creativity is limited and our success is minimal.

If we are willing to admit that we are capable of bringing negative potential to a situation, and we are willing to acknowledge our motivation behind choosing to cart argumentativeness with us to a scheduled experience, then it is possible for us to intentionally choose a different demeanor. As long as we are open to recognizing that we are a mix of potentialities, then we can take responsibility for deciding to place our most positive attributes at the base of our actions.

Once we choose to step forward with our most positive intellectual, emotional, psychological, and spiritual potentials, we can offer the circumstances our most powerful insight and interject our most effective actions. And this is when our potential is truly potent.

OUTER DISCOMFORT INDICATES INNER STRIFE

Does Your Demeanor Give You Away?

We all have times in our life when we are not sure if we want to share our problems with our family, friends, and co-workers. Our privacy is important to us. So we intentionally choose to keep a personal secret from those who care about us.

But in keeping our own confidences, we aren't always able to keep our behavior and our moods consistent. Often as we process the changes to the circumstances of our daily lives, our demeanor gives a hint to our emotional struggles. If our temperament gives rise to concern from others, are we willing to accept their caring and allow it to ease our burden? Or do we insist on grappling with our internal war alone?

Our intimate concerns can disrupt our concentration and preoccupy our minds, causing us to unintentionally disconnect from those who care about us. Sometimes it is absolutely necessary to check out of our relationships to process the changing dynamics of our own life. But at other times, it might be in our best interest to reach out and allow someone to take our hand.

When this happens our closest and most trusted friends and loved ones may intuit a change in us and ask us, "Are you ok?" We can always say yes and leave it be, because we feel sad, or embarrassed, or afraid to ask for assistance. Or we could say that we are not feeling our best. In taking this risk, we might find that the next question we are asked is, "What do you need, name it, and it is yours."

LIMITS SHIFT AND BOUNDARIES BEND

What Makes You Alter Your Stance?

The word "never" is a dangerous companion. There are times in our lives when we actually believe that we can use this word with conviction. I will never steal, I will never have an abortion, I will never get married, I will never have children, I will never get divorced, I will never live in the city, country, or suburbs, I will never have an affair, I will never cut my hair, I will never…EVER…

And yet, at any given time in our life we can be faced with a set of facts that might turn our "never" into a "maybe" or even a "yes." We can be placed inside of a scenario that we "never" imagined could be our circumstances, and then be required to rethink our insipid refusal to take part in a particular decision or action.

The Universe does this to us on purpose and at random. We are continually called upon to reevaluate ourselves and our choices. In doing so we are made to face our fears, make new choices, trust our faith, believe in fate, and hop a train to a destination that we did not anticipate. As a result we gain a new awareness, and we are moved to change and to grow into the next phase of who we are meant to be.

When we shift our limits and bend our boundaries, we arrive at a new place in our life. We might be alone, or with our old friends, or we might be with people who are new to us. Our family might have come along with us, but sometimes not. Yet wherever we land, and whomever joins us, we know that we have begun a new stage in our plan. We are ready to expand.

OVERINDULGE IN LOVE

Are You Conservative With Your Love?

What is your concept of love? Do you like to say "I love you"? Will you say it frequently and with wild abandon to anyone who raises the feeling within you? Do you require people to earn your love? Do you want something in return for giving your love?

Our culture does not embrace love. We are fearful of showing love. Many of us will not say "I love you" unless we have heard it expressed to us first. We are afraid to love.

But what does it feel like to give love away with no expectation of a return on our investment?

It Feels Like…
Ice Cream On A Beautiful Spring Afternoon
The Calmest Place In The World
Warm Sunshine On Your Face
A Place To Stay Forever
The Thing To Do
Holding Hands
Exhilarating
Courageous
Freeing
Joyous
Fun

It is…
Our Highest Truth
Our Greatest Gift

RESISTANCE IS THE HALLMARK OF GREAT SOUL GROWTH

How Long Will You Hold The Door Closed?

Change…
The inevitable altering of the landscape of our lives
Resistance…
The desire to maintain the status quo
Life…
The never ending process of transformation

Our purpose as a soul is to attempt to clear our plate of the items we chose at the buffet of growth. But the array of selections we made can seem daunting once they have taken form in the here and now. Suddenly we aren't sure if we want to participate in our chosen path toward maturing, and we attempt to turn and run from the experiences we selected. And very often, the bigger the lesson, the faster our pace in the opposite direction.

STOP! Don't sprint from your choices. You picked this journey for a reason. There is a wisdom you want to gain; a new level of consciousness that you aspire to include in your repertoire of experiences. You want to change.

THINK! Slow down and contemplate what it is you have to gain by moving through this event rather than skirting around the happening of it. Consider becoming a part of the landscape. Reduce your resistance.

MOVE! Step into the challenge gracefully and with enthusiasm. You are ready. Life is going to renovate you.

BE SMART...REACH BACK

Are You Opposed To Receiving Kindness?

Of course not. No one is. Really? Are you sure? How do you accept kindness? Do you welcome it openly and graciously, or do you receive kindness with skepticism, or uncertainty, or hesitancy, or disbelief? Do you believe that kindness is only given in exchange for it's return? Have you ever turned your back on kindness because you were afraid it would require something from you that you did not want to give?

Regardless of what we are willing to admit, many of us are suspicious of kindness. We watch those among us who seem to freely distribute affection and assistance and we wonder what their motive is. These people reach out over and over again, with seemingly no expectation of a return on their investment. What are we supposed to do with that?

We are supposed to reach back. When we step forward to receive goodness, we balance the life force around us. By reaching back and accepting the offer of thoughtfulness, we say thank you to the person who extended themselves to us. This simple act of gratitude, is gift enough. It allows the giver to complete an act of unselfish benevolence, and it allows the receiver to bask in the benefits of being cared about.

When we feel cared about, we heal and grow and gain compassion and give empathy. In doing so we change ourselves and our perspective, and the world around us is altered by our softness.

Now We Are Smarter

ANXIETY IS THE MANIFESTATION OF OUR FEARFUL THOUGHTS

Do You Think Your Fears To Life?

We cannot be afraid of the past, it has already happened. We cannot be afraid of the future, because it has not happened yet. However we can create a scenario for the future, that instills fear in our present.

When we create a negative circumstance that has not yet come into being, we are living through our anxiety. In living through our anxiety we color our immediate moment, and alter its truth. We can no longer see the current day clearly because we are preoccupied with viewing the future through a skewed lens.

By allowing our ball of anxiety to twist and turn our perception of the present, we emit our fears into the universe and compel them into being. We become a magnet for our worst nightmare.

Many of us believe that we cannot control manifesting our anxiety in this manner. But we can. By using conscious thought and staying in the madness of the moment, we can eliminate the futility of fearing the future. If we remain focused on the current minute and its immediate needs, we will be able to use our best judgment and take the most sensible action to propel us forward. We can then leave the past behind us, handle our present, and allow our future to create itself in its most perfect form.

GIVE TIME...TIME

Is Patience A Virtue Or A Process?

Some of us are old, and our idea of immediate gratification is Sanka. Others of us are young, and our idea of an instantaneous reward is Google. Regardless of how we like to order our rapid satisfaction, we are a society that rarely waits for results.

But we can still find ourselves in a place of waiting. And when we do, we have choices to make. Will we wait and stagnate? Will we wait and contemplate? Or will we wait and take the small amount of action that is available to us?

If we decide to wait and stagnate, then our outcome might not be what we are hoping for, and we will not have grown in the process. If we decide to wait and contemplate, then our outcome might not be what we are hoping for, but at least we will have given the circumstances some thought. But if we wait and take the small amount of action that is available to us, even if it is nothing more than a positive attitude, then we have allowed the energy to continue to flow, and the outcome could be a pleasant surprise.

Because in the realm of life and the Universe, it is inevitable that we will be called upon to wait for our answers. There is no immediate delivery of our desires, or our cherished outcomes. We are often forced to tread water in places we would rather not be, while we fantasize and yearn for easier days and restful nights. It is during these times that we are challenged with yielding to time, and trusting the process of our soul plan.

LEAN INTO THE UNANTICIPATED AND EXPERIENCE THE UNEXPECTED

How Mutable Are You?

Do you have a plan? Is it a plan for today, tomorrow, or the next 5 years? How strictly do you adhere to your expectations? What do you do when you realize that your path is being altered? Are you willing to flow, or do you flail in an effort to thwart the ride down the river?

We all have dreams, goals, and anticipations. Without these desires we have no direction. We use these pathways to define ourselves and measure our level of success, both personally and professionally. These structures create a sense of safety and outline our purpose in life.

From this vantage point we proceed to conquer the steps that bring our plans to fruition. We become educated, we become employed, we become entwined with other people and create the world that we envision for ourselves.

And then we are faced with an event that jars us off of our charted course. We are often startled by such a happening and react in defense of our predetermined choices. We refuse to flow. We begin to flail. Life becomes painful.

We Need To Learn To Float…To Be
Calm
Accepting
Changing

LIFE IS ALL ABOUT THE SMALL MIRACLES

What Amazes You?

Friendship
The Sun, Time, A View
A Baby, Morning, Fun, Ice Cream
The Wind, A Kiss, Color, The Ocean, A Dream
Holding Hands, Kindness, An Open Door, A Smile
Heartfelt Gifts, A Good Story, A Hug, A Piece of Chocolate
Growth, Your Sleeping Child, The Smell Of Fresh Laundry, Peace
Music, The Sparkle In An Eye, Laughter, Paying It Forward, Abundance
Competition, Art, Your Brain, Food, A Comfortable Pair of Shoes, Hats
Dance, Popcorn, The Movies, Learning, Giving, Compassion, Sand
Ice, The Perfect Pair of Jeans, A Good Hair Cut, A Picnic, Tea
A Comfortable Couch, Rain, The Smell Of Fresh Cut Grass
Flowers, Bedtime, Hummingbirds, Your Body, Stars
Fireworks, Campfires, Hot Chocolate, Hamburgers
Love, Forgiveness, Losing 5 Pounds, The Moon
Seashells, Trees, The Swings, Concerts
Diamonds, Sunsets, Starfish
Seahorses, The Tarot
Singing, Crying
Patience

GRATITUDE IS A GIFT...BE OPEN TO RECEIVING IT

Do You Know How To Accept A Thank You?

Compliments...we all crave them. A comment acknowledging that we are smart, or kind, or attractive, or helpful, raises our self esteem. A show of appreciation increases our self confidence and gives us a sense that what we bring to the world is important. So why do we shy away from praise? Why do we whisper "thank you" rather than speak proudly in our acceptance of adulation? Are we afraid to be adored?

We all impact our surroundings. As each day passes we have the opportunity to make an impression on those who we encounter. But we usually think of making a difference as something that requires an action rather than a statement. And yet sometimes, a response is more significant than a deed.

When we are open to accepting the gratitude of another, we benefit by feeling successful. When we feel successful, we participate in the joy of the moment; the joy that is derived from another individual telling us that we have improved the quality of their day. Our achievement then becomes incorporated into who we are, and we have a greater understanding of our self worth.

A life that is improved by the assistance of another, and the gratitude that is given in exchange for that betterment, completes the circle of successful giving and receiving.

Accept The Praise, Say Thank You

HOPE IS ABOUT
HARMONY   OPPORTUNITY   PEOPLE
AND
EXPERIENCES

Can The Components Of Hope Sustain You?

Harmony;

Is the intricate balance between our soul plan and our free will. When we are in harmony with ourselves and our path, we participate in the world with consistency and certainty.

Opportunity;

Is the opening that the Universe brings to us with each new event that we encounter. It is our choice whether to accept the challenges that are delivered to us, and promote our growth.

People;

Are the sources for our continued learning and human expansion. Through our relationships with other people we encounter pain and joy, creating our wholeness.

Experiences;

Are the foundation of our ability to change. We are touched and altered with each set of circumstances we engage in.

When we hope we agree to accept that we do not have control over every outcome that we desire. We place our faith in the synchronicity of the Harmony, the Opportunity, the People, and the Experiences that define our existence.

When We Hope, We Live Our Trust.

REMOVE THE OBSTACLES

Will You Allow The Details Of Your Dreams To Change?

What are your dreams? Where do they originate from? Do your dreams define you? How do your dreams impact and motivate you? Are you creating your dreams? If you encounter obstacles to your dreams, what do you do?

Dreams come from two different origins, our personal passions and our disappointments. When we engage in what we love and what brings us joy, it makes our heart race and solidifies our sense of ourselves. It is the excitement of being involved in our passions, that makes our adrenaline flow and our pulse quicken. Inside of a split second, we feel the urge to run headlong into our joy. This is the manifestation of the dreams that we create for ourselves from the core of our own uniqueness. It is through these moments that we gain a sense of wholeness and strength.

But can our dreams also be born out of our disappointments? If we lose something significant to us; a competition, a family member, a career, or a relationship, can we still see our dreams through a forced alteration? At this pivotal juncture, do we let our dreams go because they no longer look the way we anticipated they would, or do we have the courage to accept that our dreams might look slightly different now? Can an obstacle be used to create a hunger to achieve a new look for our dreams? Are we open to the same end dreams with different players, or different styles, or different names?

In the face of change we can still find our dreams, because it is our desires that create our dreams. It is our choice to believe that the core of our dreams still belongs to us. But to do this, we have to make a decision. If we want the chance to say, "My vision is still mine to live," then we have to be willing to start with something different than what we had originally hoped for. We have to see that we can make more for ourselves from an obstacle, that appeared to create seemingly less. When we remove the obstacle we discover that the vision of our future is still ours to chisel out of the world around us. The path to our dreams